CYBERSECURITY 101: A COMPREHENSIVE GUIDE TO PROTECTING YOUR DATA

by

RICHARD REYES

TABLE OF CONTENTS

INTRODUCTION

In an increasingly interconnected world, where the boundaries between the physical and digital realms blur, the need for robust cybersecurity measures has never been more critical. As technology continues to advance at a rapid pace, so do the methods employed by cybercriminals to exploit vulnerabilities and infiltrate systems. In "Cybersecurity 101: A Comprehensive Guide to Protecting Your Data," readers embark on a journey into the intricate landscape of digital security, equipped with essential knowledge and practical strategies to safeguard their most valuable asset – their data.

This comprehensive guide serves as a beacon of light in the murky waters of cyberspace, offering readers a clear and concise roadmap to navigate the complexities of cybersecurity. Whether you're an individual seeking to protect your personal information, a small business owner safeguarding sensitive client data, or a seasoned IT professional responsible for fortifying organizational defenses, this book provides invaluable insights and actionable steps to mitigate risks and thwart cyber threats.

At its core, "Cybersecurity 101" is more than just a guide – it's a call to action. In an age where data breaches and cyber attacks dominate headlines, the need for cybersecurity awareness and preparedness has never been greater. Whether you're a digital novice or a seasoned expert, this book serves as an indispensable companion on your journey to safeguarding your digital assets and preserving your peace of mind in an ever-evolving digital landscape.

Chapter 1: Introduction to Cybersecurity

In the digital era, where technology pervades every aspect of our lives, cybersecurity stands as the bedrock upon which trust and reliability in digital interactions are built. This chapter serves as a foundational exploration into the multifaceted realm of cybersecurity, elucidating its significance, delineating common threats, and outlining fundamental principles essential for establishing a secure digital environment.

1.1 Defining Cybersecurity:

Cybersecurity encompasses the array of measures, practices, and technologies employed to safeguard digital systems, networks, and data from malicious cyber threats. It encompasses a holistic approach to risk management, encompassing preventive, detective, and responsive strategies aimed at mitigating vulnerabilities and defending against unauthorized access, data breaches, and disruptive cyber attacks.

1.2 Importance of Cybersecurity in the Digital Age:

In an era characterized by ubiquitous connectivity and unprecedented reliance on digital technologies, the importance of cybersecurity cannot be overstated. From personal privacy to national security, virtually every aspect of modern society is inextricably intertwined with the digital domain, rendering individuals, organizations, and governments vulnerable to a myriad of cyber threats. The ramifications of cybersecurity breaches extend far beyond financial losses and reputational damage, encompassing potential disruptions to critical infrastructure, compromise of sensitive information, and erosion of public trust.

1.3 Overview of Common Cyber Threats and Vulnerabilities:

Understanding the landscape of cyber threats is paramount to developing effective cybersecurity strategies. This section provides an overview of common threats and vulnerabilities encountered in the digital realm, including but not limited to:

- Malware: Malicious software designed to infiltrate systems, steal data, or cause damage.

- Phishing: Social engineering attacks aimed at deceiving users into divulging sensitive information.

- Ransomware: Malware that encrypts files or locks systems, demanding ransom for decryption or restoration.

- Insider Threats: Malicious or negligent actions by authorized users posing a risk to data security.

- Zero-day Exploits: Vulnerabilities in software or hardware unknown to the vendor, exploited by attackers before a patch is available.

By familiarizing oneself with these threats and vulnerabilities, individuals and organizations can better assess their risk posture and implement proactive measures to mitigate potential risks.

In essence, this introductory chapter sets the stage for a comprehensive exploration of cybersecurity, laying the groundwork for readers to delve deeper into the intricacies of securing digital systems, networks, and data. As technology continues to evolve and cyber threats proliferate, a solid understanding of cybersecurity fundamentals is indispensable for safeguarding the integrity, confidentiality, and availability of digital assets in an ever-changing digital landscape.

Chapter 2: Fundamentals of Cyber Hygiene

In the digital realm, maintaining good cyber hygiene is akin to practicing basic personal hygiene in the physical world – it serves as the first line of defense against a multitude of cyber threats. This chapter delves into the essential principles of cyber hygiene, encompassing best practices and habits aimed at fortifying the security posture of individuals and organizations alike.

2.1 Password Management Best Practices:

Passwords serve as the primary means of authentication in digital environments, yet they are often the weakest link in cybersecurity defenses. This section explores best practices for creating strong, unique passwords and safeguarding them against unauthorized access. Topics covered include:

 - Creating complex passwords: Utilizing a combination of uppercase and lowercase letters, numbers, and special characters.

- Avoiding common pitfalls: Steering clear of easily guessable passwords, such as dictionary words or sequential patterns.

- Implementing password policies: Enforcing password length and complexity requirements, as well as regular password changes.

- Password storage solutions: Utilizing password managers to securely store and manage credentials across multiple accounts.

2.2 Importance of Software Updates and Patches:

Software vulnerabilities represent low-hanging fruit for cyber attackers, providing entry points for exploitation and compromise. This section emphasizes the critical importance of applying timely software updates and patches to mitigate known vulnerabilities. Key points include:

- Understanding the software lifecycle: Recognizing the phases of software development, deployment, and support.

- Patch management best practices: Establishing procedures for identifying, testing, and deploying software patches in a timely manner.

- Automating update processes: Leveraging automated tools and systems to streamline the patch management process and ensure prompt remediation of vulnerabilities.

- Risks of unpatched software: Illustrating the potential consequences of neglecting software updates, including increased susceptibility to cyber attacks and data breaches.

2.3 Secure Web Browsing Habits:

The web serves as a gateway to vast amounts of information and resources, yet it also harbors numerous threats in the form of malicious websites and online scams. This section provides guidance on adopting secure web browsing habits to minimize the risk of encountering malicious content. Key considerations include:

- Verifying website authenticity: Checking for HTTPS encryption, valid SSL certificates, and reputable domain names.

- Exercising caution with downloads: Avoiding downloading files from untrusted sources and verifying the integrity of downloaded files using checksums.

- Implementing browser security features: Enabling pop-up blockers, disabling auto-fill and auto-complete features, and configuring privacy settings to limit tracking.

2.4 Email Security and Phishing Awareness:

Email remains one of the most common vectors for cyber attacks, with phishing attacks posing a significant threat to individuals and organizations alike. This section explores strategies for enhancing email security and recognizing phishing attempts. Key topics include:

- Identifying phishing red flags: Recognizing suspicious sender addresses, spelling and grammatical errors, and requests for sensitive information.

- Verifying email authenticity: Validating sender identities using digital signatures, domain authentication, and email authentication protocols such as SPF, DKIM, and DMARC.

- Exercising caution with email attachments and links: Avoiding opening attachments or clicking on links from unknown or untrusted sources, and verifying their legitimacy before taking action.

By adhering to the principles of cyber hygiene outlined in this chapter, individuals and organizations can significantly reduce their exposure to cyber threats and enhance their overall cybersecurity posture. Just as regular handwashing and cleanliness are essential for maintaining physical health, practicing good cyber hygiene is paramount for safeguarding digital well-being in an increasingly interconnected world.

Chapter 3: Understanding Encryption and Authentication

In the digital age, where data traverses vast networks and resides on myriad devices, the principles of encryption and authentication serve as pillars of trust and security. This chapter delves into the intricacies of encryption and authentication, illuminating their role in safeguarding sensitive information and ensuring the integrity of digital communications.

3.1 Basics of Encryption and Decryption:

Encryption is the process of converting plaintext data into ciphertext using mathematical algorithms, rendering it unintelligible to unauthorized parties. Decryption, conversely, involves reversing this process to convert ciphertext back into its original plaintext form. This section elucidates the fundamental concepts of encryption and decryption, including:

- Symmetric vs. asymmetric encryption: Contrasting symmetric-key algorithms, where the same key is used for both encryption and decryption, with asymmetric-key algorithms, where separate public and private keys are employed.

- Encryption algorithms: Exploring common encryption algorithms such as Advanced Encryption Standard (AES), Rivest-Shamir-Adleman (RSA), and Elliptic Curve Cryptography (ECC), along with their strengths and applications.

- Key management: Addressing the challenges associated with securely generating, storing, and exchanging encryption keys, including key length, key distribution, and key rotation practices.

3.2 Different Types of Encryption Algorithms:

Encryption algorithms come in various forms, each with its own strengths, weaknesses, and applications. This section provides an overview of different types of encryption algorithms and their characteristics, including:

- Block ciphers vs. stream ciphers: Contrasting block ciphers, which encrypt data in fixed-size blocks, with stream ciphers, which encrypt data bit by bit or byte by byte.

- Public-key cryptography: Explaining the principles behind asymmetric encryption, where separate public and private keys are used for encryption and decryption, respectively.

- Hash functions: Introducing cryptographic hash functions used for data integrity verification and digital signatures, such as SHA-256 and MD5.

3.3 Importance of Digital Signatures and Certificates:

Digital signatures play a vital role in verifying the authenticity and integrity of digital documents and communications. This section explores the concept of digital signatures and their reliance on cryptographic algorithms, as well as the role of digital certificates in establishing trust and authenticity. Key topics include:

- Digital signature process: Detailing the steps involved in creating and verifying digital signatures, including hashing, encryption, and decryption.

- Certificate authorities (CAs): Explaining the role of CAs in issuing digital certificates, validating the identity of certificate holders, and maintaining certificate revocation lists (CRLs).

- Public key infrastructure (PKI): Describing the framework for managing digital certificates and public-private key pairs, including certificate issuance, distribution, and revocation processes.

3.4 Two-Factor Authentication and Multi-Factor Authentication:

Traditional password-based authentication mechanisms are susceptible to various attacks, including brute force attacks and credential stuffing. This section explores the concepts of two-factor authentication (2FA) and multi-factor authentication (MFA) as means of enhancing authentication security. Key points include:

- Two-factor authentication: Explaining the concept of 2FA, where users are required to provide two forms of authentication (e.g., password and SMS code) to access a system or service.

- Multi-factor authentication: Expanding upon 2FA, MFA incorporates additional authentication factors such as biometric data (e.g., fingerprint or facial recognition) or hardware tokens (e.g., smart cards or USB keys).

- Benefits and challenges: Discussing the advantages of 2FA and MFA in bolstering authentication security, as well as the usability and implementation challenges associated with deploying multi-factor authentication solutions.

By gaining a deeper understanding of encryption and authentication principles, individuals and organizations can leverage these foundational concepts to safeguard sensitive information, protect digital assets, and establish trust in an increasingly interconnected world. Just as the lock and key have long served as symbols of security in the physical realm, encryption and authentication mechanisms form the cornerstone of digital security in the modern age.

Chapter 4: Securing Your Devices

In today's interconnected world, where digital devices are ubiquitous and pervasive, securing these devices against cyber threats is paramount to safeguarding sensitive data and ensuring the integrity of digital interactions. This chapter explores essential strategies and best practices for securing a variety of devices, including computers, smartphones, tablets, and Internet of Things (IoT) devices.

4.1 Protecting Computers and Laptops:

Computers and laptops serve as the primary workstations for many individuals and organizations, making them prime targets for cyber attacks. This section delves into the best practices for securing computers and laptops against a myriad of threats. Key considerations include:

 - Installing and updating security software: Deploying antivirus, anti-malware, and firewall software to detect and prevent malicious activities, and ensuring timely updates to defend against emerging threats.

- Enforcing access controls: Implementing strong password policies, limiting administrative privileges, and enabling disk encryption to prevent unauthorized access to sensitive data.

- Securing remote access: Utilizing virtual private network (VPN) solutions to encrypt remote connections and protect data transmission over public networks.

- Regular system maintenance: Performing routine maintenance tasks such as disk cleanup, software updates, and hardware inspections to ensure the smooth operation and security of computer systems.

4.2 Securing Smartphones and Tablets:

Smartphones and tablets have become indispensable tools for communication, productivity, and entertainment, yet they also pose unique security challenges due to their portability and connectivity features. This section outlines the best practices for securing smartphones and tablets against various threats. Key topics include:

- Device encryption: Enabling device encryption to protect data stored on smartphones and tablets from unauthorized access in case of loss or theft.

- App security: Exercising caution when downloading and installing apps, avoiding untrusted app stores, and regularly updating apps to patch security vulnerabilities.

- Remote wipe and tracking: Configuring remote wipe and device tracking features to remotely erase data and locate lost or stolen devices in the event of theft or loss.

- Biometric authentication: Leveraging biometric authentication methods such as fingerprint recognition or facial recognition to enhance device security and user authentication.

4.3 Best Practices for Securing IoT Devices:

The proliferation of Internet of Things (IoT) devices has brought unprecedented convenience and connectivity to our lives, but it has also introduced new security risks and vulnerabilities. This section explores the best practices for securing IoT devices and mitigating potential risks. Key considerations include:

- Changing default passwords: Immediately changing default passwords upon device setup to prevent unauthorized access and exploitation by malicious actors.

- Updating firmware and software: Regularly checking for and applying firmware and software updates to patch known vulnerabilities and improve device security.

- Network segmentation: Segmenting IoT devices onto separate network segments to isolate them from critical systems and minimize the impact of potential compromises.

- Implementing network security measures: Deploying firewalls, intrusion detection systems (IDS), and network monitoring tools to detect and block malicious activities targeting IoT devices.

By implementing the security measures outlined in this chapter, individuals and organizations can significantly enhance the security posture of their devices, mitigate the risk of cyber attacks, and protect sensitive data from unauthorized access and exploitation. In an era where digital devices have become integral to everyday life, securing these devices is essential for preserving privacy, maintaining trust, and safeguarding against emerging cyber threats.

Chapter 5: Network Security Essentials

In the interconnected landscape of the digital world, networks serve as the backbone of communication and data exchange, facilitating seamless connectivity across diverse devices and platforms. However, with this connectivity comes inherent security risks, as cyber threats lurk at every virtual corner, ready to exploit vulnerabilities and compromise sensitive information. This chapter delves into the essential principles of network security, equipping readers with the knowledge and tools needed to fortify their networks against a wide range of cyber threats.

5.1 Understanding Network Architecture:

A solid understanding of network architecture forms the foundation upon which effective network security strategies are built. This section provides an overview of network components, topologies, and protocols, including:

- Network components: Explaining the roles of routers, switches, firewalls, access points, and other network devices in facilitating data transmission and communication.

  - Network topologies: Describing common network topologies such as star, bus, ring, and mesh, along with their advantages and limitations in terms of scalability, reliability, and security.

  - Network protocols: Introducing key networking protocols such as TCP/IP, DNS, DHCP, and HTTP/HTTPS, and their roles in facilitating communication and data exchange over networks.

5.2 Firewalls and Intrusion Detection/Prevention Systems:

Firewalls and intrusion detection/prevention systems (IDS/IPS) play a crucial role in defending against external and internal threats by monitoring and controlling network traffic. This section explores the principles and functionalities of firewalls and IDS/IPS solutions, including:

  - Firewall types and configurations: Contrasting stateful and stateless firewalls, as well as host-based and network-based firewalls, and discussing best practices for firewall rule configuration and management.

- Intrusion detection vs. intrusion prevention: Distinguishing between intrusion detection systems (IDS) and intrusion prevention systems (IPS), and explaining their respective roles in identifying and mitigating malicious activities on networks.

- Signature-based vs. anomaly-based detection: Comparing signature-based detection, which relies on predefined patterns or signatures of known threats, with anomaly-based detection, which identifies deviations from normal network behavior.

5.3 Secure Wi-Fi Configurations and Best Practices:

Wi-Fi networks have become indispensable for providing wireless connectivity in homes, businesses, and public spaces, yet they also present security challenges if not properly secured. This section outlines best practices for securing Wi-Fi networks and mitigating potential risks, including:

- Strong encryption: Configuring Wi-Fi networks with strong encryption protocols such as WPA2 or WPA3 to protect data transmission from eavesdropping and interception.

- Network segmentation: Segmenting Wi-Fi networks into separate VLANs or SSIDs to isolate guest networks from internal networks and minimize the impact of potential compromises.

- Access control measures: Implementing measures such as MAC address filtering, captive portals, and Wi-Fi Protected Setup (WPS) to restrict access to authorized devices and users.

- Regular security audits: Conducting periodic security audits and vulnerability assessments to identify and remediate security weaknesses in Wi-Fi network configurations.

5.4 Virtual Private Networks (VPNs) for Secure Remote Access:

In an era where remote work and telecommuting have become increasingly prevalent, virtual private networks (VPNs) play a crucial role in ensuring secure remote access to corporate networks and resources. This section explores the principles and functionalities of VPNs, including:

- VPN types and protocols: Comparing different types of VPNs such as site-to-site VPNs, remote access VPNs, and SSL VPNs, along with common VPN protocols such as IPSec, L2TP/IPSec, and SSL/TLS.

- VPN deployment considerations: Discussing factors to consider when deploying VPN solutions, including scalability, compatibility, performance, and security requirements.

- VPN security best practices: Implementing measures such as strong encryption, multi-factor authentication, and secure VPN gateways to protect VPN connections from interception and unauthorized access.

By mastering the essentials of network security outlined in this chapter, individuals and organizations can build robust defenses against a wide range of cyber threats, safeguarding their networks, data, and digital assets from malicious actors. In an era where network breaches and cyber attacks pose significant risks to businesses and individuals alike, investing in network security is essential for preserving confidentiality, integrity, and availability in the digital age.

Chapter 6: Defending Against Malware

In the ever-evolving landscape of cybersecurity threats, malware remains a persistent and pervasive menace, capable of wreaking havoc on digital systems, compromising sensitive information, and disrupting critical operations. This chapter delves into the intricacies of malware, equipping readers with the knowledge and tools needed to defend against these insidious cyber threats.

6.1 Understanding Malware:

Malware, short for malicious software, encompasses a broad category of software programs designed to infiltrate, damage, or steal data from computer systems and networks. This section provides an in-depth exploration of different types of malware and their characteristics, including:

- Viruses: Self-replicating programs that attach themselves to legitimate files or programs and spread from one system to another, often causing damage or data loss.

- Worms: Standalone programs that spread across networks by exploiting vulnerabilities in operating systems or applications, often with the intent of causing disruption or facilitating unauthorized access.

- Trojans: Malicious programs disguised as legitimate software, which trick users into executing them, thereby granting attackers unauthorized access to systems or compromising sensitive information.

- Ransomware: Malware that encrypts files or locks systems, demanding ransom payments in exchange for decryption keys or system restoration.

6.2 Preventing Malware Infections:

Prevention is key to mitigating the risk of malware infections and minimizing their impact on digital systems and data. This section explores proactive measures and best practices for preventing malware infections, including:

- User education and awareness: Training users to recognize common signs of malware infections, avoid suspicious websites and email attachments, and report potential security incidents promptly.

- Implementing security software: Deploying antivirus, anti-malware, and anti-exploit solutions to detect and block malware infections in real-time, and ensuring regular updates to maintain efficacy against emerging threats.

- Patch management: Applying timely security patches and software updates to address known vulnerabilities and reduce the risk of exploitation by malware.

- Secure browsing habits: Exercising caution when browsing the web, avoiding clicking on malicious links or ads, and using ad blockers and script blockers to mitigate the risk of drive-by downloads and exploit kits.

6.3 Detecting and Removing Malware:

Despite best efforts to prevent malware infections, no system is immune to compromise. This section explores strategies and techniques for detecting and removing malware from infected systems, including:

- Malware scanning and detection: Conducting regular malware scans using antivirus and anti-malware tools to identify and quarantine malicious files and programs.

- Incident response procedures: Establishing incident response plans and procedures for responding to malware infections, including isolating infected systems, collecting forensic evidence, and initiating remediation efforts.

- Malware removal tools: Leveraging specialized malware removal tools and utilities to safely and effectively remove malware from infected systems without causing further damage or data loss.

- System restoration and recovery: Implementing backup and disaster recovery solutions to restore infected systems to a clean state and minimize the impact of malware infections on critical data and operations.

By adopting a proactive approach to defending against malware and implementing robust security measures, individuals and organizations can mitigate the risk of malware infections and safeguard their digital systems, data, and assets from malicious actors. In an era where malware threats continue to evolve and proliferate, vigilance and preparedness are essential for maintaining the integrity and security of digital   environments.

Chapter 7: Protecting Your Online Identity

In an increasingly digitized world, where personal and professional interactions occur predominantly online, safeguarding one's online identity is paramount. This chapter explores the complexities of online identity protection, providing readers with essential strategies and best practices to mitigate the risk of identity theft, fraud, and unauthorized access.

7.1 Privacy Considerations in the Digital World:

Privacy is the cornerstone of online identity protection, yet it is often compromised in the pursuit of convenience and connectivity. This section delves into the importance of privacy in the digital realm and offers guidance on preserving privacy online, including:

- Data minimization: Limiting the collection and sharing of

personal information to only what is necessary for legitimate purposes, and exercising caution when providing sensitive data to online services and platforms.

- Privacy settings and controls: Reviewing and configuring privacy settings on social media accounts, online profiles, and digital devices to restrict access to personal information and control how it is shared with others.

- Privacy-enhancing tools: Utilizing privacy-enhancing browser extensions, VPNs, and encryption tools to anonymize online activities, protect sensitive communications, and prevent tracking by advertisers and data brokers.

7.2 Social Engineering Attacks:

Social engineering attacks represent a significant threat to online identity security, relying on manipulation and deception to exploit human psychology and gain unauthorized access to sensitive information. This section examines common social engineering tactics and provides guidance on recognizing and thwarting such attacks, including:

- Phishing: Identifying phishing emails, messages, and websites designed to trick users into divulging sensitive information or downloading malware, and adopting phishing awareness training programs to educate users on recognizing and avoiding phishing attempts.

- Spear phishing: Distinguishing spear phishing attacks, which target specific individuals or organizations using personalized messages and social engineering techniques, and implementing email authentication protocols such as SPF, DKIM, and DMARC to mitigate the risk of email spoofing.

- Social media manipulation: Recognizing social media scams and hoaxes designed to exploit users' trust and curiosity, and exercising caution when interacting with unfamiliar or suspicious accounts and content on social media platforms.

7.3 Identity Theft Prevention Tips:

Identity theft remains a pervasive threat in the digital age, with cybercriminals constantly devising new tactics to steal personal information and perpetrate fraud. This section offers practical tips and recommendations for preventing identity theft and safeguarding sensitive information, including:

- Strong authentication: Enabling multi-factor authentication (MFA) wherever possible to add an extra layer of security to online accounts and prevent unauthorized access in the event of stolen credentials.

- Secure password management: Using strong, unique passwords for each online account, and storing them securely using password managers to mitigate the risk of credential reuse and password guessing attacks.

- Monitoring credit reports: Regularly monitoring credit reports and financial statements for suspicious activity, and promptly reporting any unauthorized transactions or discrepancies to financial institutions and credit reporting agencies.

- Shredding sensitive documents: Shredding physical documents containing sensitive personal information before discarding them to prevent dumpster diving and identity theft.

7.4 Safeguarding Personal Information Online:

Personal information is a valuable commodity in the digital economy, sought after by advertisers, data brokers, and cybercriminals alike. This section explores strategies for safeguarding personal information online and minimizing the risk of unauthorized access and exploitation, including:

- Limiting data exposure: Exercising caution when sharing personal information online, avoiding oversharing on social media, and being selective about the information provided to online services and platforms.

- Data encryption: Encrypting sensitive communications and files using encryption tools and protocols such as SSL/TLS, PGP, and

BitLocker to protect data in transit and at rest from eavesdropping and interception.

- Data breach response: Developing a plan for responding to data breaches and security incidents, including steps to take immediately following a breach, notification procedures for affected individuals, and resources for identity theft victims to mitigate the impact of stolen data.

By implementing the strategies and best practices outlined in this chapter, individuals can take proactive steps to protect their online identities, preserve their privacy, and mitigate the risk of identity theft and fraud in an increasingly digital world. In an era where personal information is both a prized asset and a potential liability, vigilance and awareness are essential for maintaining control over one's online identity and ensuring its integrity and security.

Chapter 8: Data Backup and Disaster Recovery

In the digital age, where data serves as the lifeblood of businesses and individuals alike, ensuring its availability, integrity, and confidentiality is paramount. This chapter delves into the critical importance of data backup and disaster recovery, providing readers with essential strategies and best practices to safeguard their data against loss, corruption, and unforeseen disasters.

8.1 Importance of Regular Data Backups:

Data loss can occur due to a variety of reasons, including hardware failures, software errors, human error, cyber attacks, and natural disasters. This section emphasizes the importance of regular data backups as a foundational strategy for mitigating the risk of data loss and ensuring business continuity, including:

- Reducing downtime: Minimizing the impact of data loss on operations and productivity by maintaining up-to-date backups of critical data and systems.

- Protecting against ransomware: Thwarting ransomware attacks by restoring encrypted data from backups rather than paying ransom demands, thus denying attackers their leverage.

- Compliance and regulatory requirements: Fulfilling legal and regulatory obligations related to data retention, archiving, and protection by implementing robust backup and recovery processes.

8.2 Choosing the Right Backup Solutions:

Selecting the appropriate backup solutions and strategies is essential for ensuring the reliability, scalability, and security of data backups. This section explores different types of backup solutions and considerations for choosing the right approach for specific needs and requirements, including:

- On-premises vs. cloud backups: Contrasting traditional on-premises backup solutions with cloud-based backup services, and evaluating factors such as cost, scalability, accessibility, and security.

- Full, incremental, and differential backups: Understanding the differences between full, incremental, and differential backup methods, and selecting the most suitable approach based on data volume, frequency of changes, and recovery time objectives (RTOs) and recovery point objectives (RPOs).

- Backup retention policies: Establishing retention policies to determine how long backup data should be retained and how frequently backups should be performed, taking into account legal, regulatory, and business requirements.

8.3 Disaster Recovery Planning and Preparedness:

Effective disaster recovery planning is essential for minimizing the impact of catastrophic events and ensuring the rapid restoration of critical systems and data. This section provides guidance on developing comprehensive disaster recovery plans and procedures, including:

- Risk assessment and business impact analysis: Identifying potential threats and vulnerabilities, assessing their potential impact on business operations, and prioritizing recovery efforts based on criticality and severity.

- Recovery time objectives (RTOs) and recovery point objectives (RPOs): Defining RTOs and RPOs to establish recovery timeframes and data loss tolerances for different systems and applications, and aligning disaster recovery strategies accordingly.

- Backup testing and validation: Regularly testing and validating backup and recovery processes to ensure their effectiveness and reliability, and identifying and addressing any gaps or weaknesses in the disaster recovery plan.

8.4 Testing and Validation of Backup Procedures:

Regular testing and validation of backup procedures are essential for ensuring the integrity, reliability, and effectiveness of backup and recovery processes. This section explores best practices for testing and validating backup procedures, including:

- Scheduled testing: Establishing a schedule for conducting routine backup tests and validation exercises, and documenting the results to identify areas for improvement and refinement.

- Scenario-based testing: Simulating different disaster scenarios and recovery scenarios to assess the readiness and resilience of backup and recovery processes under various conditions.

- Automation and orchestration: Leveraging automation and orchestration tools to streamline backup testing and validation processes, reduce manual intervention, and ensure consistency and repeatability.

By implementing robust data backup and disaster recovery strategies outlined in this chapter, individuals and organizations can mitigate the risk of data loss, minimize downtime, and ensure business continuity in the face of unforeseen events. In an era where data is both ubiquitous and vulnerable, proactive measures to safeguard data integrity and availability are essential for maintaining trust, resilience, and competitiveness in the digital age.

Chapter 9: Incident Response and Cybersecurity Incident Management

In the dynamic landscape of cybersecurity, incidents are an inevitability rather than a possibility. How organizations respond to these incidents can make the difference between swift containment and widespread damage. This chapter delves into the essential principles of incident response and cybersecurity incident management, equipping readers with the knowledge and tools needed to effectively detect, respond to, and recover from cybersecurity incidents.

9.1 Developing an Incident Response Plan:

An incident response plan serves as a roadmap for how an organization will detect, assess, contain, and recover from cybersecurity incidents. This section explores the key components of an incident response plan and provides guidance on developing and implementing a comprehensive plan, including:

- Incident detection and reporting procedures: Establishing mechanisms for detecting and reporting cybersecurity incidents, including incident response team roles and responsibilities, escalation procedures, and communication channels.

- Incident classification and prioritization: Developing criteria for classifying incidents based on severity, impact, and urgency, and prioritizing response efforts accordingly to minimize the impact on critical systems and data.

- Response procedures and playbooks: Documenting step-by-step response procedures and incident response playbooks for different types of incidents, including malware infections, data breaches, denial-of-service attacks, and insider threats.

- Coordination with external stakeholders: Establishing partnerships and communication channels with external stakeholders such as law enforcement agencies, regulatory bodies, and third-party vendors to facilitate coordination and information sharing during incident response efforts.

9.2 Detecting and Responding to Cybersecurity Incidents:

Timely detection and response are critical for containing cybersecurity incidents and minimizing their impact on business operations and data integrity. This section explores strategies and best practices for detecting and responding to cybersecurity incidents effectively, including:

- Real-time monitoring and alerting: Implementing continuous monitoring solutions and security information and event management (SIEM) systems to detect anomalous activities, indicators of compromise (IOCs), and security incidents in real time.

- Threat hunting and analysis: Proactively searching for signs of malicious activity and potential security threats within network traffic, system logs, and endpoint data, and conducting in-depth analysis to identify the root cause and scope of incidents.

- Incident containment and eradication: Taking immediate action to contain and eradicate cybersecurity incidents, including isolating affected systems, disabling compromised accounts, and removing malicious files and software.

- Forensic investigation and evidence preservation: Conducting forensic investigations to collect and preserve digital evidence related to cybersecurity incidents, and documenting findings for legal, regulatory, and internal review purposes.

9.3 Post-Incident Analysis and Lessons Learned:

Post-incident analysis is essential for identifying gaps and weaknesses in incident response procedures and improving the organization's overall cybersecurity posture. This section explores the importance of post-incident analysis and provides guidance on conducting comprehensive post-mortem reviews, including:

- Root cause analysis: Identifying the underlying causes and contributing factors that led to the cybersecurity incident, including technical vulnerabilities, human errors, and process deficiencies.

- Lessons learned and best practices: Documenting lessons learned from cybersecurity incidents and incorporating them into incident response playbooks, policies, and procedures to prevent similar incidents from occurring in the future.

- Continuous improvement and refinement: Establishing a culture of continuous improvement by regularly reviewing and updating incident response plans, conducting tabletop exercises and simulations, and staying abreast of emerging threats and attack techniques.

By implementing effective incident response and cybersecurity incident management practices outlined in this chapter, organizations can minimize the impact of cybersecurity incidents, mitigate risks, and enhance their resilience to cyber threats. In an era where cyber attacks are on the rise and the stakes have never been higher, a proactive and well-coordinated approach to incident response is essential for safeguarding critical systems, data, and operations.

Chapter 10: Ethical Hacking and Penetration Testing

In the ongoing battle against cyber threats, organizations must adopt a proactive approach to identify and mitigate vulnerabilities before malicious actors exploit them. Ethical hacking and penetration testing serve as invaluable tools in this endeavor, allowing organizations to assess their security posture, identify weaknesses, and implement effective security controls. This chapter explores the principles and practices of ethical hacking and penetration testing, providing readers with insights into how these techniques can be leveraged to enhance cybersecurity defenses.

10.1 Understanding Ethical Hacking:

Ethical hacking, also known as penetration testing or white-hat hacking, involves simulating cyber attacks on systems, networks, and applications to identify vulnerabilities and security weaknesses. Unlike malicious hackers, ethical hackers operate with the consent and authorization of the organization to improve its security posture. This section delves into the principles and methodologies of ethical hacking, including:

- Scope and rules of engagement: Defining the scope of ethical hacking activities, specifying the systems and assets that are authorized for testing, and establishing rules of engagement to ensure compliance with legal and ethical guidelines.

- Reconnaissance and information gathering: Conducting reconnaissance activities to gather information about the target environment, including network infrastructure, system configurations, and application architecture.

- Vulnerability assessment and exploitation: Identifying security vulnerabilities and misconfigurations using automated scanning tools and manual techniques, and exploiting these vulnerabilities to demonstrate their impact and severity.

- Reporting and remediation: Documenting findings in a comprehensive report, including detailed descriptions of vulnerabilities, risk ratings, and recommended remediation measures to address identified weaknesses.

10.2 Types of Penetration Testing:

Penetration testing encompasses various methodologies and techniques tailored to assess different aspects of an organization's security posture. This section explores the different types of penetration testing and their respective objectives, including:

- External penetration testing: Assessing the security of externally-facing systems, such as web servers, email servers, and VPN gateways, from the perspective of an external attacker attempting to gain unauthorized access.

- Internal penetration testing: Evaluating the security of internal networks, systems, and applications from the perspective of an authenticated user with insider privileges, including testing for lateral movement and privilege escalation.

- Web application penetration testing: Identifying security vulnerabilities and weaknesses in web applications, such as injection flaws, cross-site scripting (XSS), and insecure direct object references, to prevent data breaches and unauthorized access.

- Wireless network penetration testing: Assessing the security of wireless networks and devices, including Wi-Fi access points, routers, and mobile devices, to identify vulnerabilities and weaknesses that could be exploited by attackers.

10.3 Best Practices for Ethical Hacking and Penetration Testing:

Ethical hacking and penetration testing require careful planning, execution, and oversight to ensure accurate and reliable results. This section explores best practices and considerations for conducting ethical hacking and penetration testing engagements, including:

- Clear objectives and goals: Defining clear objectives and goals for the penetration testing engagement, including specific targets, testing methodologies, and success criteria.

- Documentation and reporting: Documenting all activities, findings, and observations throughout the penetration testing process, and preparing detailed reports for stakeholders that prioritize identified vulnerabilities and provide actionable recommendations for remediation.

- Collaboration and communication: Fostering collaboration and open communication between penetration testing teams and organizational stakeholders, including IT staff, security teams, and executive leadership, to facilitate knowledge sharing and decision-making.

- Continuous improvement: Incorporating lessons learned from penetration testing engagements into the organization's security strategy and practices, and continuously refining and enhancing security controls and defenses to address emerging threats and vulnerabilities.

By embracing ethical hacking and penetration testing as essential components of their cybersecurity strategy, organizations can proactively identify and remediate vulnerabilities, strengthen their defenses, and minimize the risk of data breaches and cyber attacks. In an era where cyber threats continue to evolve and proliferate, ethical hacking and penetration testing serve as indispensable tools for staying one step ahead of adversaries and safeguarding critical assets and infrastructure.